CW01498958

Purpose Blueprints : complete your mission ease and grace.

To my son, Shiloh, I am so very proud of you for living your Divine Destiny Blueprints 100% each and every day. You are such a wise soul here on Earth. Through your example of you listening to your gut instincts and what your soul is guiding you to do, you have navigated your Soul's Calling brilliantly... At only 21 years of age! You are living your Divine Life Purpose way earlier than I did and with much less fumbling around. For this I am so very thankful. You being fully aligned with why you came to this planet in the first place was one of my biggest prayers for you when I gave birth to you.

May you always know how deeply you are loved Shiloh. You have amazing Divine Gifts and your clients are so blessed to have the privilege of receiving your Soul's Gifts you so abundantly share with them.

To my Dad & Jeanie, cheers to your

dedication to living a life of health, peace, longevity and ease of being. May you continue to experience bliss, higher health blueprints, joy, love and deep peace during your retirement years. Thank you for blessing my life with strength of being, and family love. Living near you here in Silver City, New Mexico helps me with fulfilling my Soul's Calling each and every day.

My son Shiloh and I

44 Days of Archangel Messages That Activate Your Soul's Calling

44 Days of Archangel Messages That Activate Your Soul's Calling

Kimberly Dawn

The Archangels

44 Days of Archangel Messages That Activate Your Soul's Calling © Kimberly Inc.. All Rights Reserved, except where otherwise noted.

Dedication

I dedicate this book to Archangel Michael
and all of the Archangels who spoke
messages through me so they could bring
you, the reader an over lighting of love and
healing as you read the passages in this
book.

I thank all of the Angelic Counsels of light
who will be working with you on a soul
level as you read the Archangel messages
designed on the higher Angelic realm to
activate your Soul's calling to the next
level you are ready for at this time.

I also dedicate this book to you, our most
beloved reader. May your Soul's Calling
be activated with your highest Life

Lovely Angel Visit

I woke up to the most beautiful vision this morning (in a half sleep state) to an Angel I saw in the driveway. He had the most beautiful long blonde hair and gave me the most profound message that confirmed my life's work. He completely touched my heart. When these visitations from Angels happen they alter us in some way... They are an activation from the Divine Realm of God. Usually some type of change comes after these visits, a slight altering of our pathway happens or a huge one. We create our own heaven on earth one person at a time. Just know that you are so loved and cherished right where you are.

My Prayer for You and Your Life...

Thank you for loving yourself enough to give yourself the gift of reading this book and all the blessings and activations that come through it from the Archangels and their healing teams.

I know you were led to find this book for a reason. May you receive an enormous amount of love, abundance, prosperity, Divine wisdom and miracles before, during and after reading the Archangel messages in this book they had me type specifically for you. There are messages for your life that the Archangels will bring you. There are activations and blessings while you read these words that contain light codes that you need at this time from the Divine and your soul.

May the light of you know how deeply you are loved.

May your Soul's Calling be activated 100% upon reading these passages. You are led to read each day as you open this book to the very message you are in line to read that day.

May the blueprints for your Life Purpose, Divine Destiny, Soul's Calling unfold with ease of being and through grace most of all.

In Love and Grace,

My Prayer for You and Your Life...

Disclaimer

I, Kimberly Dawn, am not a medical doctor and do not practice medicine. I don't diagnose, heal, cure or treat disease. I recommend people continue to see their medical doctors and follow their advice. My work and Archangel Crystal Light Energy Healing is a complement to conventional medicine. The theory behind these treatments is that the body develops blockages in its energy field and disease or imbalances are the result. These treatments are designed to eliminate those blockages so that energy can flow more freely through the body. Spiritual Energetic work theory believes when one's energy field is in balance; the body's latent healing ability can heal itself. I make no promises or guarantees about the results of this work.

A Facebook Post I Wrote After the Launch of My First Book, "365 Days of Archangel Messages"

Yay! Book sales are going good on Amazon. That's the best feeling in the world... Knowing I am fulfilling my Soul's Calling on earth with the Archangels being able to touch the lives of more around the world. It's not about the sales for me, it is about being able to reach many more souls that the Angelic realms want to bring more light to.

It took so many years for them to heal me enough to be able to know what my life purpose was, so that I could actually complete it. Never stop believing in the whispers of light you are hearing each and every day. The faint, yet strong whispers of "go here, take a small step today...". They are the very things that add up to creating a feel good, joyful life from the inside out.

I believe it is the lulls or the dips in life that help us redefine what our joy truly is. I'm thankful for the constant redefining of what will bring more joy, love, peace and expansion with the help of the Angels daily.

We don't do any of this alone, we have so much higher support, guidance and nurturing that is here for us. Now we can actually hear it and feel it more since more light grids have been placed all around the planet from the Ascended Masters, God's Light, the Angels, the Archangels, and the Saints.

Hopping off the old ways of doing things, the old grids that are on the earth, onto the new blueprints... the light grids that are now here for us may be scary at times because it means changing the way we are doing things, but is so worth the journey. Sometimes we fall down, but what awaits is only more joy as we ride the freedom waves of higher light grids the Angelic realms are bringing us though Divine Grace.

Your Soul's Calling is Your Birthright

Helping you activate that reason is part of why I came to this planet.

By reading the Archangel messages in this book you'll be working with them ethereally to activate your Divine Soul's calling. For as long as you own this book the Archangels and their healing teams assure me that you will be able to open this book and navigate to any printed or digital page and receive more of your Soul's Calling activations through reading any Archangel Message that you are drawn to read that day.

Message from Archangel Michael:

"Before you decided to be born through your Mother Earth you pre-designed your highest mission of service that you wanted to come to earth to do. These plans, these blueprints were discussed and often times redesigned with your Soul and the Angelic Counsels of Light that work with soul's before they incarnate into a physical body here on earth. Often times alternate plans (blueprints) are mapped out based on meeting certain people or encountering obstacles that may occur along your path.

Whenever there is a tragedy that occurs or a cataclysmic event in a person's life, that soul will usually call upon the very same Counsels of Light that helped them design their Life Purpose, Soul's Calling blueprints before they incarnated to redesign them based on the circumstances that have just occurred. This continues to happen throughout a person's life as they are willing.

This happens while they sleep and ethereally with their higher aspects of that person's soul.

As you read the passages in this book Kimberly has brought through from myself and all of the Archangels the higher aspects of you will be working with the Angelic Counsels of Light that helped you design your Soul's Calling before you came there.

You being drawn to read this book means you are a treasured member of a light team of the highest accord who has come to earth to be of service, by bringing higher light activations to the planet. Sometimes your ability to receive the higher light codes from us have been blocked by the denseness and the chaotic energies that happen on this planet.

We have asked Kimberly to bring through the messages in this book so we may reach those of you who need these blocks undone and transformed with your higher templates and blueprints brought in and activated for you by us and all of your Angelic Counsels of light. Part of Kimberly's mission is to be that receiving end for us, so that the transmissions she receives by us can then be activated with the specific light codes you are needing at this time for your

Divine Destiny blueprints. Your next level of your Soul's Calling to be able to come in for you all the way without obstruction.

We have a very specific light team that is extremely proficient with transforming any obstructions, blocks or stresses you are facing in your life so that your Divine Mission may be lived with ease and grace. It is our honor to assist you in this way through the passages in this book that have been very carefully brought through by Kimberly.

May all you wish to glean from this book be made so.

You will feel our light teams working with you in ever increasing amounts as you request our assistance and navigate to any message in this book. It is our honor to be by your side strengthening your light so that you may live the rest of your days in Divine peace, love, joy, bliss and witness many miracles of obstacles being removed from your pathway with the ease of 2000 Saints and Angels bringing in Divine Light on your behalf.

Indeed, you are worthy of this and more.

We love you infinitely and forever.

Yours truly,

Saint Archangel Michael"

A Reason to Make a Difference

I am so thankful for my life. I have been majorly sensitive most of my life, painfully so. Wasn't until age 40 I was able to fully step into my Soul's Calling and use my soul's gifts to help others with theirs. I've never been happier.

I believe we are in a time on earth where it is essential for the planet and for many to carve out our life's work and let it mold itself into the highest and best way to help those we are meant to serve with our soul's gifts. I had to do many different entrepreneur businesses to build the business skills I needed, such as web design and even real estate.

The negative side of my gifts is that sometimes it

is painful for my brain to be too social and chat a lot with others for the sake of making small talk. My brain just wants to be one with the Divine and the Angels most often, yet I love my family and close friends – they even know I need my "oneness" time.

I am just so appreciative at this stage in my life I can channel my energy into my creations and reach those the Archangels and healing team want to reach through me. It's not always easy to find one's Soul's Calling... It took me many renditions of mine to fine tune it. I had many so called "failures" along the way, but that is part of it.

You must not be afraid to create and create some more. I am so thankful today that I have the privilege of living my Soul's Calling 100%. If you are sensitive with some things in life, just know that it can be turned into major fuel for your life's work. It's a fun ride when we allow ourselves to be fully who we are in the world without apology. You are made different for a reason.

Day 1 Archangel Michael

"To begin anew each day with clear focus sets the tone for ease and flow with each stepping stone. If you feel disjointed upon awakening, try taking a gentle or brisk 5 – 10 minutes' walk or laying down upon Mother Earth and simply letting go for a few moments. Call us in as you do this and ask us to clear anything that may be blocking you from having a creative, prosperous, abundant, flourishing day. What brings peace to your heart will unfold your unique creative ideas exactly as they are supposed to. Reward yourself at the end of the day with a good read or an enlightening movie. You deserve all the replenishing segments life has to offer."

Day 2 Archangel Metatron

"It is overwhelming when road blocks step in, because your brain simply needs more rest. Taking moments of allotted downtime to let your mind wander fills up your momentum again. Also, implementing ideal times in your day when your creative flow is the highest in order create, do your art or express yourself in writing helps your team of writing Angels know when to show up to bring your ideas and inspiration. When self-doubt arises as to if you can get it all down, chunk it down into just this hour. When are you inspired to do this hour? What would you like to get done in the next hour that will bring you the most peace tonight when you fall asleep? Do this and reward yourself with some time in nature, even if only for 5 minutes afterwards. Let nature reward and refuel you or reset your pace for what comes next. You don't have to think too far ahead, only one hour at a time planning is enough to finish your projects. Eventually, they will complete themselves with you having plenty of sun fuel left over."

Day 3 Archangel Ariel

"Having a role model that falls short has happened to so many of the greatest authors and citizens in the world. Many, many have looked up to Oprah as a most wonderful role model. It is very helpful during the creation process to have a role model to look up to. Think about one you've had in your past that hasn't lived up to the expectations you wished they had. What qualities did you wish they had, that they fell short of? This quality ranks high on your list as a sacred value, does it not? When you have a sacred value like this and a certain leader struggles with this value, if you are called, you may want to step into more of a leadership role with this value you hold near and dear to your heart. When it comes to your creations, how can this sacred value be called forth to assist your creative ideas to be expressed with ease and grace? Close your eyes if you choose and listen, sense or feel into the answer for you. How else can you amplify this value to become more a part of your world and creation process? This is something that is right for you through and through. We bring your support, more strength and ease of being around this area. What you intended with this sacred value becoming more a part of your life with enhancing your creativity we bless today with our love. This area is anointed for you, and so it is."

Day 4 Archangel Raphael

"Sometimes your greatest pain, holds within it stories and lessons you can impart within your art, your creative expression. For instance, think of a pain you have in your body or you recently had. Ask it what wisdom it has to share with the world and see what it says. How may you impart this wisdom with your readers? Jewels of wisdom are contained within each painful event of life that holds the antidotal power to transform that core misalignment for all of humanity. Let the wisdom flow from you like the Nile river. The reach of your golden jewels of understanding can create offshoots like the branches of the tree of life. The fruit your tree bears holds the love within them to bring life to all the nations upon the earth."

Day 5 Archangel Gabriel

"Forgive yourself for your past misunderstandings of truth. What hurt you and held you back in your past does not need to be erased. Think about one area you wish you would have done differently in your past right now. Now picture your ideal reader, what would you like to share with your reader that would have made a big impact upon your life if you would have done that area of life differently? It is also good to note, how are you allowing this area of your life to be much easier now? It is in the effortless flow of your life that the real diamonds are found.

Ask us to help you forgive all parts of yourself tonight that did so-called mishaps and those parts of yourself that walked blindly into traps in your past. While you sleep tonight we will be working with you forgiving all parts of self that went off on some unfavorable tangents. We will help these areas heal, feel loved, know that all is going to be okay and integrate them into wholeness again. May the love of you supersede all of the regret and doubt. What comes next is really, really Divine."

Day 6 Archangel Michael

"Interruptions may be blessings in disguise. Sometimes they just happen to keep you more on target. Your schedule may be different than anyone else's around you. When your time gets impeded upon stop and ask us what next task would bring you peace. You may be surprised by the answer. Go forth in alignment that all is working in your favor, not against it. What brings you peace today places gems of peace inside your creative ideas. Let your insights rein free in those peaceful moments. What they will reveal to you are jewels of wisdom for your writing."

Day 7 Archangel Metatron

"Let the urgency you feel turn into waves of creative love from the deepest, most passionate part of your being. To underestimate your ability is not conducive to the flow of who your soul already is. If someone shall reject you and this hurts, call us in to help you see, feel and know just how much you are a diamond in the rough. The jewels of wisdom inside of you already are plentiful. The more you share them the more bounty they'll bring you in return. What delivers your love brings it to other's hearts too. Share what you know. Be willing to get it wrong. There is someone wanting the very lessons of love you have to impart to them within your writing. Remember this, every creative idea you have holds the potential of easing the suffering of twenty people. Imagine how many lives will blossom from each creative expression you place into the world. Let the timeless journey of writing continue forth. Trust the flow and rhythm of your creative ideas and let them sing to your ears and heart. Listen for the beat of what wants to come next. Your journey has only just begun."

Day 8 Archangel Ariel

"In your hands we place a lotus flower today. This lotus flower holds the blueprint for your highest Destiny for your art. Now, place this lotus flower in your heart when you are ready and know that only good will come from your inspired ideas reaching all whom it is meant to touch with your most beautiful expressions from the heart. Let your heart play a song for you today. Listen for the beat and let it ripple through your fingertips with effortless river flow magic. All who are drawn to drink from your life giving works of art will be called. May your heart be at peace with how easy writing is for you. May you have a twinkle of magic in your eyes as you smile to those who cross your path."

Day 9 Archangel Metatron

"When you receive interruptions from certain people at those precision times you need to get into your creative flow, we'd like you to look at these situations as an opportunity to stop and smell the roses so to speak. Sometimes taking longer breaks than you think you can afford, helps you recharge your batteries so that when you come back to your writing, it has more grit to it. Life challenges seek hold on ebb and flow. When the tide feels like there is an ebb, we'd like you to go with it and allow yourself the much needed downtime of rest that your body and brain are calling out for. Sometimes to "force" the flow to go a certain way leads to confusion and less clarity. To gain the maximum clarity and endurance the athlete must rest up before the race. When sprinting is needed you'll be so relieved you took those moments to allow complete renewal of your body, mind and spirit. Call us in during these times to send your faculties quantum light fields of rejuvenation. You may be pleasantly surprised what's waiting for you on the other side. As you receive our Angel light fields of love you'll be light years ahead of where you thought you'd be in only a few months' time. Resting gets you further ahead with the encoded light support you'll receive."

Day 10 Archangel Michael

"What helps in prioritizing your schedule and your to-do items is knowing when you feel most inspired to work. What works for some, such as doing their most creative work first thing in the morning may not work as well for you. You might find that after a mid-day nap is when you are most creatively inspired to do your best work. Ask us to assist you with your prioritizing ritual. We will highlight for you the best times of day to do all your tasks. You may find by flip-flopping some tasks around with regard to the time of day you do them and adding more resting time during your low energy hours, you'll be invigorated with a renewal like you've never had before.

What comes first is giving yourself permission to rearrange your schedule so brings you joy instead of dread. We love to see you look forward to your most creative tasks. What also helps is taking yourself off the hook with tasks that you can delegate or ask others to do for you in exchange for paying them or offering them a service you love doing. We often see that those who begin brightening 10% of their day with some of these practical light enhancing techniques are able to build a joyfully expansive momentum that picks up speed and fun time."

Go to ArchangelsBless.com to receive FREE Archangel Messages anytime day or night. Ask a question, receive an answer.

Day 11 Archangel Raphael

"If you find that your digestion at certain times of the day is bothered more than other times, we'd like to work with you on this to bring your stomach area more peace. To know what kind of food enhanced your focus long term without upsetting your digestion helps. What also may be the trigger is more loving energetic boundaries for yourself. We'll be working with you tonight while you sleep to assist your digestion and your energy level so that your creative ideas process becomes as sweet as pie. When your digestion smooths out, so too does your life, they go hand in hand. As your life feels more nurturing to you on all fronts your digestion and cravings get more evened out. What would help you feel absolutely loved before going to sleep at night? Write about this as you feel drawn and see what comes up for you. We'll meet you in your dreamtime with the love you have been craving."

Day 12 Archangel Gabriel

"Nurturing your ideas by jotting them down, one by one, helps us bring in more blueprints for each idea you have. When you are curious about how to expand upon an idea call me in to assist you. Your ideas on the etheric planes are real, living, breathing holographic images and shapes that contain miniscule blueprints of light that can be expanded for each and every idea into profound and most joyous earthly creations here in the physical. To bring your ideas fully into the material world, into matter, the first step is writing them down. The ideas that still light you up to look a couple weeks to a month from now contain seeds of learning for you to explore. Sometimes it isn't just about making an idea into a certain end point, but it may be more about going through the learning process with that idea and allowing it to show you what it wants to expand into. If you are scratching your head over this, just know to follow the trails that light you up with a feeling of grounded connection can be the most life enhancing of all. What rests as ideas in the palm of your hands, often times are the very ideas that feel like the sweetest, sunshine filled ride yet."

Day 13 Archangel Ariel

"When you believe something is possible, infinite worlds of possibilities open up around that obstacle you once deemed impossible. The reality you bring into this world out of the multitude of pure potentials that exist depends upon how clear your looking glass is. The choices that sparkle the most with hope, love, tenderness and the ones that leave you with a feeling of vibrant warm fuzziness inside is the one to go with. Could more choices down the road present themselves that are even better? Indeed, they can and often do. In order to get to those long-shot choices it is most important to make the best possible decisions that you are presented with today, you see? The longer you put off until tomorrow the longer tomorrow gets. If it has been put on the back burner for quite some time, the longer your dreams manifest into form. In order to draw to the ultimate dreams you have, ask yourself, what projects can I complete this week or this month that would help me feel crystal clear again? Usually the very things we keep pushing to the side are the very things that would remove the roadblocks to our higher Divine Destiny manifesting quite magically and with much less effort than we expected. Prune the trees dragging your Divine Destiny down and watch the resolutions roll in day after day."

Day 14 Archangel Gabriel

"Let your heart be full of love today no matter how much you actually create. Find pleasure in the simplest of treasures today. Nothing needs to be done overnight. You have infinity at your door. Each time you step through infinities door you become something greater than before. Let your imagination wander, dance, play and simply be. You are more than you are expected to be, right here, right now. Trust your inner promptings for more play, for the fun adventure has just begun."

Day 15 Archangel Michael

"Self-doubt creates an unfair playing ground in your mind. One way to replace self-doubt is to picture yourself in your favorite garden or location on earth that feels like "heaven" to you. Then proceed with writing one sentence. All you need to create is the space for yourself to listen to your inner voice, listening to what it wants to say to you and seeking higher guidance from there. When you allow yourself to go to the location on earth you crave (in your mind and heart), you may find that sanctuary space fuels your creative ideas into form. When you go beyond the gates of your current reality, into a heaven on earth reality you create in your own heart, new life in the form of your artistic expression take shape without effort. Breathe deep and take your "heaven on earth" vacation in your heart and mind each time you find you have nothing to create. Pretty soon creations that are more alive than you can think up on your own begin leaping before you."

Day 16 Archangel Metatron

"When you speak to yourself with your inner dialogue be easy on yourself, for there is no higher gift to yourself than what you say in those moments when you feel no one else is listening. What you think, feel and know matters. We never second guess you, we only offer you golden streams of inspired visions. When you are worried about what you'll get out of your art or creative expression, this may stifle them before they even have a chance of blossoming flowers for you to enjoy. Pretend you have an audience of millions about to view your creative work and this was your last year on earth. What would you say to your audience of millions before you leave the planet? If this was your last work of writing you leave as your gift to mankind, what would you want them to hear and feel deep within them? Go there, be with that golden light wave of all that is good. Ride that golden light beam all the way through 'till your writing feels like a well spring of golden treasures. As you create from this space, all that is supposed to be said will. There is no need to predetermine your Soul's Calling with exact precision... Allow it to take you on a magical journey of wonder each and every day. Looking forward to the journey in this way brings infinite divinely inspired written word journeys ahead."

Day 17 Archangel Raphael

"Breathe deeply as you sit down to allow the creative juices to flow, for it is through breathing that the creative ideas flow more freely. When in doubt, call me in. For it will be no time and you will sense how your art wants to be expressed through you. Your genius lies within your ability to tap into higher resources of knowledge. Your ideas are masterpieces in the making. Allow yourself to feel guided as to when to let go, enough to be one with your inspired creations that are next to be expressed. Your genius and your ability to tap into higher sources involves a deep surrendering process of your will alone, in order to allow clear creative ideas from your soul to flow through you. Your soul sees the bigger picture and knows how to reach those who need your wisdom the most. As you breathe, you allow us to bring your wisdom light from the Angelic Realms. Think of this as a lamp in the dark of the night, helping you see clearly what wants to arrive next in your world of ideas that wish to be expressed and brought to life through you. Allowing the jewels of wisdom to come forth in this way brings deep peace to your heart, body, mind and soul. You are so endeared by us, always remember this. The creative formations that want to be born through you are powerful indeed. We thank you for being willing to surrender to a greater knowing than yourself. The enlightenment process of connection to divine sources is occurring as you bring us in to assist your inspiration – for those who you create your inspired work for and for you the creator. As your art is experienced by your audience we are bringing in frequencies of abundant blessings for them as they view it, experience it, and sample it. Creations brought in from your heart, from calling in higher light – calling in your

Soul's Calling blueprints will always be mesmerizing to those who are drawn to your art and creative expressions. There are Divine Light Codes of Love coming in for you right now as you read these words. The same goes for what you bring through as you call upon us, the Archangels to assist. What you invent, create, encapsulate holds the potential to heal all the nations of the world, even if just one seedling of those light codes get brought into form and shared with the world. Divine light codes that we place upon your pages are forever in the Akashic records and held with high regard. For you creating your art, expressing your ideas into physical, spoken or written form makes it easier for Saints being born into countries to hold the frequencies of light they came here to bring, you see? Never doubt the good you are doing with intentions to uplift others through your artistic expressions. All that is good from your heart is held of the highest accord in ours."

Day 18 Archangel Ariel

"As distractions arise, know that they are there to show you what you truly want more of in your life and what feels draining to you. Getting really clear on which one gives you energy and what distraction takes energy from you holds the key in opening the door that will bring your goals and dreams to you ever so effortlessly. Another way to decipher what contributes to your life purpose is asking the question, "Will this matter 5 years from now?" If the answer is no, you'll know how much weight to give that thing that is trying to grab your attention. By clarifying what will make an impact to your Soul's Calling in this way helps you decide what to prioritize next. Also, you may call me in to ask me to assist you with deciding whether something demanding your attention right now is worth giving your time to. Close your eyes and feel deep within your being, what is pulling on you right now? Now ask me to help you feel, hear or see whether this will add to your life 5 years from now. What do you sense? Keeping a notebook next to your bed at night is helpful to jot down anything that comes to you so you can remember upon awakening. Often times we bring your inspired thought and resolutions while you are resting. That which brings you the most peace is your answer. May the clarity that comes to you set your heart and soul free to focus your time and attention on what ultimately matters most."

Day 19 Archangel Raphael

"As you are entering into a brand new blessed cycle, call us in to smooth the way for you, to usher in light from the Angelic Kingdom from behind the scenes. Things no longer have to be difficult any longer. What lies ahead is smooth transitions of expanded life blueprints that have been designed especially for you, you see? What brings these easier life blueprints in is by your request. Anytime you ask for our assistance for anything and for your writing to happen effortlessly we work with your soul to create a blueprint for what you have requested so that when you begin work on that area of life things will effortlessly happen for you that brighten your day. Let today and each day forward be a new day. What brings you clarity, peace and harmony helps your new blueprints come in. You do indeed have what it takes, you always have. We are assisting you with having faith in the tiniest of actions daily towards your dreams. It is in the minute faithful; feel-good actions you are inspired or prompted to take daily that your dreams unfold with magical ease of being. Let yourself know all is well by knowing deep inside your being that you ARE WORTHY of what you most desire. There is no other way around it, you were born for this."

Day 20 Archangel Michael

"Often times when you hear ringing in your ears it is us and your healing team adjusting the frequencies all around you so you may hear, feel, see and sense messages of inspiration easier. Ethereally your creations, your art has already been created on the higher realms by your soul – this is how the visions and inspired thoughts come to you in the first place. Call upon us, all of the Archangels bring frequencies of light of the highest accord into all of your cells, body, mind and spirit while you sleep. It is here your art gets pre-created and receives Divine Blessings for an effortless writing process from all of us. Trust what's coming to your fingertips to type onto the pages. What interrupts your flow is lack of trust in the entire creative, ebb and flow process. To create your art, your expression through love first, the feeling of love in your heart makes an impact upon your viewer as they experience it. What brings you comfort and a sweet feeling to bring through gives their heart wings of love, so they may feel not so alone in the world. Speaking directly into the soul of the reader comes from relaxing into your own well-spring of creative love you hold for yourself. As you deliver unto yourself daily what you wish another would do for you, you fill up your vessel with lighted inspired ideas of hope – creations that hold the potential of enhancing your audience's lives forever. When you doubt yourself, you stick a fork in this process and impede upon your soul's cherished creations your soul wants you to birth. As you play more, knowing all is Divinely aligned ahead of time by you and with us, you open the floodgates of heaven with rainbows appearing with messages of joy waiting for you to relish in them."

Go to ArchangelsBless.com to receive FREE Archangel Messages anytime day or night. Ask a question, receive an answer.

Day 21 Archangel Gabriel

"Celebration abounds for your earth journey of love and adventure. As you celebrate the smallest of accomplishments more inspiration flies in upon a butterfly's wings in simple moments of tuning in. Close your eyes if you'd like. We hand you a white gift wrapped box for you to open today. Within this box is a message for you that holds within it light codes to assist your creations to be fully born in the highest light expression possible. See what your message is now by opening your gift from us and seeing, sensing or feeling what it is. You may want to write what you saw, felt or heard down on paper, for it will bring you many magical blessings for your writing process. Do this exercise as often as you'd like to receive more blessings for your life. You deserve these gifts of light from us and the Divine. What awaits is pure gleeful joy and effortless abundance, prosperity and more sweet times filled with love. May your heart expand into the lotus flower it is meant to become. You are enough our sweet child. What you desire has been blessed by us."

Day 22 Archangel Jophiel

"Have faith that you are being called to create your inspired ideas for a reason. This is a new season for you and it is time for you to claim what you are worth as well as what you are here to do on this planet. As you remember more and more why you came to earth, your desires come to fruition easier. What you dream of is real. When you mind drifts to a location on earth you'd like to travel to this is showing you what treasures await you there. Whether you travel there physically or ethereally, you are called to go there. Where your heart longs to travel to may hold the jewels of discovery waiting to enhance your light filled creations. What brings life to your writing brings life to you, there is no other way. You yearning to travel at some junctures of your life holds within it peace filled memories that lift you higher. You are ready for more travel adventures in your heart, mind, body and soul. As the time nears ripe the resources will appear, for they are near. Your life design was never to be stagnant, but always flowing where the winds and currents are taking you next. This season of your life there's lots of movement and journeys to be had. You are a cherished member of the light team sent to earth to bring important light codes to certain places and locations. You do go there while you sleep and journey in the middle of the night. You'll know the locations you are to travel to physically in this lifetime. That which brings peace to your very core brings meaning and depth to your creations you have brought into this world that last for centuries. As you write down what your dreams are, we bless them each and every day. Every last one of them. What you want to happen, has happened already. There is time and you are more than worthy in every way possible."

Day 23 Archangel Azrael

"Look inside right now and see, feel or sense what it is you might be resisting. This is an entry point of what may be holding you back. Very good. As you feel into this area I am assisting you with resolution here so that the well-spring of creation to flow more smoothly through you without obstruction. Allowing this area of your life to be healed by us brings your writing into the light of day, so that all who may benefit from the sincerest of creations expressed from your heart will be attracted to the light that comes through your inspired ideas brought into form.

This brings you into the flow of least resistance, yes? As you follow the stream of inspired thoughts the current brings you to the promised land within yourself. Your ideas are your greatest allies. One seedling of an idea cracks open to the promised land within your heart center. All of your desires are held there also. Picture yourself bathing in the freshest spring water underneath a waterfall that you can imagine. Allow all of your cells to drink this purity and clarity of purpose up through this waterfall of love. We are bathing you in frequencies now that is clearing away the obstacles energetically. That's it. Go ahead and take a swim in the clear blue pool of spring water now. Dive deeply until you arrive at the clear bottom of nature's pool and find a sparkling treasure we have left for you here. Gather it up and return to the shore. Now hold this treasure up to your ear and listen for a message in it. What does it say to you? Return to this location at any time by closing your eyes and feeling your beings drinking in the waterfall of Divine Love. The more you return to this safe space, the less worry you'll have and the more your desires will effortlessly appear before you in the most miraculous ways."

Day 24 Archangel Michael

"What prevents some from their dreams coming to fruition is old strongholds in and around the heart chakra area that need healing. The old wounds or injuries tend to collect in this area and when one makes progress towards their dreams the wounds from the past tend to close the heart chakra trying to protect it. Today we bring you healing frequencies for your heart chakra for its full transformation into Divine Light again. If you say yes, while you sleep tonight we will be healing the parts of your past that have contributed to your heart chakra closing out of a need to protect itself. When you awake you'll notice a difference in the area of your heart. Your breathing may feel more expanded and easier. Let it be knowing to the deepest part of you today that you are in fact worthy of that which you dream of. What has troubled you in the past is now being transformed into pure motivation – soul fuel. You have stood the test of time our dear friend. Now it is time for your journey back home to arrive inside your heart. What you wish for is happening now. Allow the freedom feeling that is enveloping you to lift you up all the way to the top of the mountain you are climbing. This freedom-ride is yours to partake in for eternity. You have found yourself now. Let the world hear, see and feel your freedom filled creations upon Divinity's breath."

Day 25 Archangel Chamuel

"Certain people around you may not believe in your project all the way yet. The ones around you who do not believe may want you to stay the same in order for them to be more comfortable. For many, change equals pain. The changes you are making are for the highest and best good of your soul's evolution on earth. What would be best for those around you may not be the greatest for you. We are assisting you with becoming stronger inside so that your directives from within override the messages you are picking up from those who do not understand your dreams, you see? What helps you stay focused is to free yourself from the expectations of others and know that the journey you are on may be one that is meant to expand those around you in ways they may not be fully ready for just yet, but they will be as you continue taking inspired steps each day you are led to embark upon. You were never meant to be a robot doing the same thing every day year after year. Your life design was one in which you are meant to heed the call of spirit, your soul, your higher self and go forth with love of the adventure of each day. We'd like you to recall the last great adventure you had... Remember that exquisite feeling from within that took you to place you never thought you'd go? What led you there was your soul calling you to expand, to become more of yourself. Every adventure, every great journey leads you to more of yourself and ultimately leads you back home."

Day 26 Archangel Uriel

"What brings you farther ahead is in the knowing that you may not believe your dreams at first, you may not actually believe they will come true at all. Being okay with not knowing what comes next holds the key. You quest has taken you this far and did you always know what step you were going to take before you took them or did some become obvious only as you took the first step? Did you sit for a little while pondering and relaxing into the unknown and then all of a sudden you got a sudden insight and know what your next step will be? The human journey is one of the great unknown. The journey itself requests from you a deep respect to the surrendering into the unknown, the abyss. As you allow yourself to be led in a moment by moment listening, the enormous undertaking of goals becomes a simple enjoyment process of unfolding your next joy tidbit. Like eating a Hershey's chocolate kiss. If you sat and ate the entire bag in one sitting you would not feel all too well. The same goes with unraveling all of your story at once. Allow the tidbits of time to unravel themselves. Therein lies the joy of the journey."

Day 27 Archangel Haniel

"If you are asking yourself the question, "How am I going to accomplish it all?", we'd like you to close your eyes and imagine yourself already there. You have what you dream of. The job is done. What feelings do you have upon completion? Ask your future self what helped you complete it? Take a few moments to do this inward journey if needed and we will meet you there lighting up inspired thoughts for you. You deserve all that is good. All that is good is of God. What feels good to you is for you to allow in. What doesn't feel good to you is not your higher destiny. What feels like settling for second best is coming from a distorted view point that one must give up what they value in order to survive. This survival mentality is transforming now into you receiving your higher Divine Destiny blueprints all the way now. As you sleep tonight, if you say yes, we will be bringing in more of your Soul's Divine Destiny blueprints so that your pathway will be over lighted with blessings from the Divine. What is good for you will be well lit and feel like a breath of fresh air for your soul. Your longevity and joy come from you being fully connected to your Divine Destiny blueprints so that each day you are dancing and having a blast within them, naturally and gracefully unfolding the next step in a sacred dance with the Divine. You and the Divine are one, you see? What feels "off" to you is. What feels like a full connection of yourself with your creative life force energy, IS indeed. You have come a long way our dear friend. We have assisted you the entire time. Continue to embody what feels like love and you'll be in the graceful flow all the way home."

Day 28 Archangel Metatron

"When you doubt yourself you are forgetting that you are an eternal being of light. In eternity there is no time, there is only creation at its shining glory. What seems hard can be made simple by requesting it to be so. Writing down what you'd like to happen and at the end of each line including "and let this be in the effortless flow of the Divine", brings about miraculous happenings that resolve issues before they even happen. Instead of dancing with problems, we are teaching you on the higher etheric planes that you also exist on, how your creations can be created from the effortless dance within the Divine's Love for your life. When you walk outside of this love for self is when you may have fallen on your knees in the past. What brings about change for your future in a gracious flow of least resistance is in knowing how much support and help you have from us at all times. What once caused you to flow against the tides has been shifted into a higher state of being for you now. Breathe in the knowingness that your life is about to get really, really good. You have super human abilities to be who you truly are now. Allow your internal cues to be a leeway into the higher purpose you have designed for your life with the Divine. And so it is."

Day 29 Archangel Metatron

"As doubt and fear come up to the surface every so often, we'd like you to recognize it is about the journey and not the destination. As you solidify your goals onto paper, the key ideas and visions you are seeing that you want to make happen, we invite you to look at them from the vantage point of the sweet feelings from within they will create. Instead of viewing them as a means to "get further ahead" we'd like you to view them with a softer lens. Whether you "get there" or not is not the point. What helps you stay relaxed about it all is to remain in a state of magical wonderment about how what you desire already exists in the future. To cherish the feelings of the sacred journey we invite you to be in a state of "play" with your dreams and your writing. To unfold magical moments in your now time is to remember there is nowhere to "get to". What enjoyment segments of sheer play and magical wonder can you add to your day? Exposing yourself to more of these interludes of no-time segments prepares the ground for fertile seeds to be planted in the spirit of play. As you recall what it felt like in your most exhilarating playful moments as a kid, this brings you the sense of relief you are seeking. To open up more daydreaming moments of joy like this brings in fruitful trees of nourishment you can continue to feed off of in those moments doubt arises. What precedes good writing and a life of bliss is a magical wonderland of joy interludes."

Day 30 Archangel Ariel

"Our sweet dear one, we treasure you asking us questions to help you clarify what is best for you. What brings you a sense of comfort will bring others that same feeling of comfort. We ask you today, "How can you bring yourself more comfort and joy with your creation you are working upon?" Sense what comes to you through asking your inner self this question. Wonderful work. We are so pleased to assist you with living more of your Soul's Calling in your daily life. You deserve infinite amounts of joy, peace and abundance. There is plenty of prosperity to go around. Your abundance comes from living higher and higher joy states of being... In a fun and grounded way. What you so desire is happening right now. What you wish for is already coming true. You have the ability to manifest all your desires. Be peaceful with all of it and know you are worthy of loving your dreams through love."

Go to ArchangelsBless.com to receive FREE Archangel Messages anytime day or night. Ask a question, receive an answer.

Day 31 Archangel Michael

"What helps your body, mind and soul relax is knowing it is all being taken care of for you. There is nothing to "get to". You are already there. Close your eyes and picture the most beautiful flower you've ever seen before you. Ask the flower what message it has for you today regarding what concerns you and sense, feel or hear what it has to tell you. Very good. Much more information will be brought to you through that flower's image while you sleep tonight. Know that you are right where you are supposed to be. Please know that you are doing enough. There is nothing more you should be doing. Allow your most beautiful heart to be free of burdens now. Rest assured all you are doing is more than enough. May you feel our deep love and support we bring you daily. We are right there with you each moment you think of us – sending you waves of peace frequencies so that all of the tension you are holding leaves your body. Allow your mind to be free of any worry, for all is absolutely being taken care of for you. And so it is."

Day 32 Archangel Gabriel

"To feel loved from deep within is what we aim for with you. What helps you feel deeply loved and nourished from the inside out? Where do you feel you are lacking in this area? Think about this now and place any feelings, thoughts or images of "lack" into a golden ball of light and hand it to me. I now take this ball of golden light to God, to the Divine to be healed completely. You are now being bathed in lavender, pink, white and golden light of God, of Love. You are worthy of this. You are worthy of your heart's desire through and through. This love is now bathing all parts of you that feel separate and unworthy with the wisdom light of pure potentiality. Purifying your body, mind and soul into the true essence of who you really are. What you seek shall find you in this purity – for it is already seeking you. What you ask for from this place of purity of soul, so shall it be for the highest and best good of all. May your heart feel the wholeness of your pure nature now. You are indeed a wondrous spirit of expanding enlightenment whose possibilities are endless."

Day 33 Archangel Raphael

"What has held you back before no longer needs to be so. Your light is meant to shine brightly and be a beacon of light in the midst of any darkness around you. What brings you solace is in knowing you do not need to shut your light off to make others around you more comfortable. This was never what your soul intended for you. Your purpose is to become your fullest expression of your soul you have ever had in embodiment – this means quirks and all. When others are uncomfortable from your being your Divine Self – in love with your life, it is but a cry for help on their part. They have yet to see many of their glory days. When you have an inspiration to create work from your heart, it is but an act of self-love to do so, yes? To love yourself is to cherish your soul's creations wanting to express themselves through you. To be in a hurry through life wanting to get to point Z, you miss the infinite blessings that your Soul and God have waiting for you. To be in the sheer joy of creation itself is to allow love that's knocking at your door in. All the effort that's required is to open the door. In opening the door, Divine Magic can be born through you. Indeed it is so."

Day 34 Archangel Ariel

"Life disappointments lead to inner revelations of what truly matters to your heart. In the process of excavating all the layers the pain that comes up to heal, underneath it, is a reservoir, a well-spring of divinity herself waiting to gift you with gifts of paradise on earth. When you find yourself not motivated to take action or sinking into a lull ask yourself this, "What is it that wants to express itself through me that I am not allowing?" What wants to come out, dance and play through you?... Is your greatest calling in action. You have many gifts inside of you wait-

ing to burst forth unto the play of creation herself. We hereby give you full permission to allow
them out. With the exhilaration of soul expression – your soul expressing yourself through
what comes natural to you, you bring the treasures of your soul to the earth. What you yearn
for already wants to be born through you and
from your heart of expressions. We bring you
peace today in knowing that your chosen path
does not need to be a hard one. You have already
won the battle from within. Now will you accept
the great glory of Divine Treasures that are ready
to be received by you?"

Day 35 Archangel Metatron

"As others remark on your work with subpar comments, take it as only a reflection of what's going on inside that person. They may see the world from a more limited perspective than you do and let their remarks be taken with a grain of salt. The work that wants to be born through you is here to touch millions of lives and it always has been. You are trusting the flow of what wants to come through you more and more. What helps you have faith in the work that is ahead is in knowing how vitally important it is to get your work out there. What has blocked you from placing your work out there into your reader's hands has been removed. Any resistances you have with getting the creative ideas into the world are being transformed by us with ease and grace. What once brought you pleasure may be changing because at the very essence of your being, you are becoming more likened to your Divine Self as a living embodiment of the Divine Essence herself on earth. Your cravings are being neutralized so that what matters most comes to the forefront with your work. You may find you no longer wish to do the things that used to drive you forward. What drives you into momentum now may be the love of the work itself. Instead of having anywhere to get to you are in wonderment of what wants to spontaneously come through you in each now moment you show up in curiosity. Allow planning too much for the future to be replaced by the sheer joy of creating in this moment and watching the moments like you do a brilliant sunrise. It is a site to behold indeed. Let your wonderment of life itself precede all planning."

Day 36 Archangel Michael

"What helps you feel most loved may be in resting all achievement and all goals at this time. To show up and behold the breath of life itself without having to be at any certain place in the future brings great peace of mind as you simplify what matters most to your heart of hearts. We present to you today on a silver platter a phone call from us. Pick up the phone and feel, sense or hear what we have to say to you right now, if you will. Take time to write this down as needed. We want you to know how dear you are to us. What brings you the most peace is usually the action to take that is for the highest and best good of all. We energize for you today all the blessings waiting for you to receive from the Divine, from God. Many of these blessings are far greater than your mind can conceive at this time. We are preparing the way for many miracles to be made so through your life and in the lives of all those whom you know. There is no need to chase anything anymore, not even a story. Let all come to you that is seeking your light and love. What is meant for the highest and best good of all will prevail."

Day 37 Archangel Raziel

"Distractions can be seen as a good or bad thing. We'd like you to begin noticing the distractions that are pulling at you. Write down your top 3 distractions. When you view the distractions from afar you'll notice they hold a pattern to them. The things that pull you may be trying to get your attention for a reason. We'd like you to circle the distractions that energize you and underline the ones that drain you. You may have both a circle and an underline. Which of these 3 items you listed would you like help elevating to a level in which they serve your greater good?

Double underline these. Very good. What pulls you into distraction mode, often times is trying to help you avoid something that feels painful for you to delve into. Write down the top 3 things you are avoiding. Now we'd like you to list what is the deeper pain about what you find yourself avoiding. Write any thoughts down that come to mind when you ask yourself what the deeper hurt is underneath these 3 things you tend to avoid. If you say yes, we will work with your soul and bring in deeper healing tonight as you sleep for these old wounded areas. What brings light to them trickles healing into all the lives you are meant to reach by you being your authentic self. Let what wants to be uprooted come up to the surface. Placing undue pressure on yourself will not heal the wounded parts. Bringing light and love to these areas will. We will be helping to transform those old pain grids of injury within you so you will naturally be drawn to move forward with the action you know is for your highest and best good to take. May you know that you are an extraordinary being of light. It is time to be the real you in this world. We bathe you in Divine frequencies

of Love so all your heart's desires will be mani-
fested much easier now. And so it is."

Day 38 Archangel Zadkiel

"Sometimes ideas need a bit of spring cleaning. After you read your ideas you have jotted down you may want to note the ones that make you leap for joy and flood you with song. The ones that put a smile on your face, even if they seem impossible or out of reach are the ones to focus increments of time on. To be willing to get it wrong is key here. Some ideas will be scratched off or placed to the side for now and that's okay. Circle the ones that make you want to leap out of your seat and get to them. Even if your logical mind says you cannot because you have a lot on your plate, you'll want to make some time on your days off or your mornings to "indulge". This is a very important part of being human. Knowing which items to give yourself permission to spend time "playing" with and which items feel like they pull you off your higher path and are only a distraction. Knowing the difference here will set your heart free. We give you permission to focus upon that which pleases you most even if others do not understand. How you spend your time while on earth is a very important one. What pulls you forward onto a higher pathway and feels like "play" at the same time is where to spend your time. Ultimately the gifts of heaven are here waiting for you."

Day 39 Archangel Daniel

"Sometimes negative people can drag you down, yes? When those around you feel like "Debbie downers" this brings you an opportunity to allow even more floods of creativity through to enter your being as solutions for the problems they speak about. What obstacles do you see over and over again in those that want to complain? What issues are they facing that you could solve with ingenious creative ideas? Begin writing these down – call them "antidotes for the negative ones in my life". You do not need to share this with them, only keep a log of what creative ideas want to be born through to counter-act the beliefs of what they speak of. If they hold those limiting thoughts, many others around the earth do. How your ideas can help heal 1000's is in solving problems in this antidotal method. Instead of sinking down to their level, what creative ideas could you bring to the world at large as antidotal medicine to bring healing balms to many who are suffering. When you look at the negative voices as a means of creative ideas, they stop dragging you down and they begin fueling your inspired choices and in turn bring in more soul creations that breathe more life into the world."

Day 40 Archangel Michael and all the Archangels

"To be here in this world right now is more than challenging to say the least. What has left you feeling disappointed and saddened is to be expected. Never underestimate your power of prayer. When you write down what you would like help with and ask for help in your written prayers for those whom you know and all of the world you help the more harmony on your physical planet. Did you know that one prayer alone can usher in over 1500 Angels at once from

God's throne of Angels? Yes, indeed this is true. Angels needs your prayers in order to have permission to go to work on your behalf. Your requests are a powerful form of healing for the planet. There is nothing more powerful to create healing for all than prayer requests from your sincere heart. We know it is challenging to not know if peace will rein tomorrow. Amidst the turmoil we ask you to write down your requests for more support, love, abundance, joy and healing for all. In doing so 1500 plus angels will begin going to work on your behalf and for every single item you pray about. Let it be known that this is really how it works. Amidst upheaval, prayerful light is needed for all you can think about to request and write down. Keeping a notebook on hand helps us read your passages and begin delegating more support for you for every entry written. Let your heart be free from worry – you are taken care of and supported by us. What brings your mind, body, soul and heart peace brings it to the world at large. You have taken a grand stand in claiming peace for the entire world by making your requests known to us in this way and we thank you for your courage to be here in this time of great change amongst planet earth and her people. We bring you frequencies of peace in through your heart now. Allow this peace to permeate all of your being. Indeed, you are one with the almighty Creator of all that is good. May the highest good for you and all of humanity prevail."

Go to ArchangelsBless.com to receive FREE Archangel Messages anytime day or night. Ask a question, receive an answer.

Day 41 Archangel Jeremiel

"What has been lost for centuries for some souls has caused deep pain inside of you. This deep seated sadness is coming up for release with humanity in waves... Like the ebb and flow of the ocean. What has been blocked from you for lifetime after lifetime is now shifting. The tide has turned for you and now is your time to shine and be the guiding light that you are for many. Your light has never been brighter here upon the earth and we are exhilarated for your journey into oneness in this lifetime. Much of the world is in upheaval right now. It is still best advised to only ingest into your system with your eyes and ears what is peaceful for you. Watching snippets of the news helps to get the gist of what is going on, however, prolonged viewing may cause you to feel imbalanced and unsettled. The more of you that are bringing in waves of peace the better. To heal nations first begins by bringing in peace into your bone marrow... All of your cells. With God's peace in you comes inspired action through love. To sail into the Waring sea with just one ship is too tumultuous for one to go to battle alone. To be the peace you'd like to see in the world brings peace waves and tides of joy to many. Allow all of your being-ness, mind and body to feel how much peace is prevailing around the world and amplify this feeling within you. To be that which you wish to see in the world is to create a new world from the inside out. We are endeared for your service here upon the earth, more than words can describe and we stand by your side morning, noon and night protecting you and energizing your body systems with peace frequencies of enriching love from the source – your original home-land. Let peace rain in your heart today and all that is good will come your way."

Day 42 Archangel Raphael

"So much anxiety and tension is happening in the world right now. Sensitive souls are feeling this at the very core of their bodies right now. Today I bring you healing frequencies of light to ease the anxieties and tension. For all parts of you deserve to feel peace, joy, love and sincere support. Breathe my healing light in I am sending you now. Feel it permeate all of your body, mind and soul, even into your bones, down into your toes and out the bottoms of your feet entering the center of Mother Earth herself. What brings you tranquility of mind is best for you to focus upon. What helps you know you are safe, loved and taken care of is where we'd like you to place your thoughts. We are releasing worry for you through these soft frequencies of light. Trust that everything that is happening in the world has a Divine purpose far greater than one individual mind can see. Picture, feel or sense the deepest area of concern you have right now. What troubles you we'd like you to bring this to mind now so we may bring in more assistance for you for this area of concern. Place this area of worry into a golden bubble of light and hand this to me. Very good. When you say no to what doesn't absolutely feel good to you, that which may cause you to feel "off center", you are saying yes to allowing more healing light tones of peace to reside within you and enter into our precious Mother Earth's crust and heal her as well. That's better When you call upon me to help you transcend your anxieties like this, you are playing a Divine part in healing the entire planet at large. Allow your love to shine through in all that you do. What your heart longs for is now able to reach you easier with less effort. Be in sweet peace our friend. Your wellness, abundance, love, joy, connectedness, serenity and livelihood is our top priority. We love you infinitely and forever. And so it is."

Day 43 Archangel Michael

"May you know the wonder that is you. Forgive yourself for all the times you felt you didn't "get it right". Humbly seek to know yourself, your true self. Today we are sending frequencies of light to transform all residual pain from times past. What felt so hurtful for you now holds the light code keys to set you free. As this year comes to a close, remember what is most important to your heart of hearts. To be real with yourself in this way brings bountiful blessings from God, your soul and us. At the end of your life upon this planet what makes your heart sing now will then as well. Let the benevolence of your soul gifts shine forth. Your soul would like you to now you are enough right where you are. There is nowhere to "get to". Be here now in the peaceful glory that is you and let the rain wash away any haze around you. As you say Yes, we bring you higher light coded keys of wisdom so that your journey is one of peace, forgiveness, love, tenderness, abundance in all ways and sovereignty. And so it is."

Day 44 Archangel Raguel

"When your body is physically feeling like it is resisting going to a certain location, over a friend or families house, into a group situation you aren't feeling absolutely delighted about, we'd like you to your inner promptings here. What would you rather be doing instead? The resistance is occurring to show you there often is a better way to go about things. To heal that which you came here to heal brings great peace to your body systems and helps you have a feeling of relaxed ease with your life. Your soul may be calling upon you to stop and listen to the inner promptings for more peace in your life which may mean participating with less people at times. There is a rhythm to the creative pulse of inspired ideas that are being born through you expressing them into the world. What precedes this is often more time to relax, take it easy, clear and cleanse the body, mind in soul with inspired practices of pure clean water, fresh air and life giving foods and herbs. Call upon me to help simplify your life so that you can hear us and your inner voice better. If you have a very busy life, then 5-10 minutes in the morning of personal time to meditate and listen to what higher messages are coming to you to pay attention to helps enormously! We guide you today fully into your creative freedom. You were born as a being of light upon this planet to be able to bring your ideas into the form of matter. What matters to you is indeed very important to the world. When you hold back your creative ideas for fear of them not being readily accepted you are in essence preventing more love from entering your own life. Those that may seemingly reject your work may not be your audience. In order to reach those who will love your work it is important to practice the art of creation itself

– create for the sake of creating for yourself first. What makes your heart sing while you are creating – do this, be one with this energetic pulse. The heartbeat of Mother Earth herself can be found here. Beating your creative drum for the sake of feeling the rhythm itself is indeed a very important aspect of why you were born here in the first place. Trust this, be one with your drum, sing to the highest almighty that you are ready and open to receive the inspired light from the Divine herself. Watch the magic unfold – that which wants to be delivered unto the world through you shall be with the love and grace of eternities hand."

Bonus Day 45
Archangel Azriel

"There is a place inside our Dear One where all the questions you have about the Universe reside. By going into this place deep inside your heart you will feel our healing balms of love for you and the Creator's love for you. This space inside your heart has not been tainted or damaged by life's traumas. It has been protected and kept sacred for you. To enter into this sacred space inside your heart is not a far journey it is always available for you, preserved and kept safe in God's love and light. As you journey here more often you will find deep buried treasures from your soul waiting to be discovered. These treasure chests contain all the secrets of Universal knowledge. What has held you back for so long can be dug up, excavated, released once and for all like the chipping away of the cave to discover sunlight awaits. Call us in while you journey into your sacred heart so we may meet you there and bring you your crowning glory. Here you will put the puzzle pieces together of why you journeyed to the earth in the first place. There are deeply held secrets from within that need to be released into the light of day, even if that is simply writing them down and asking us, the Archangels to release you from the burdens of these buried secrets. Once they have been brought to the surface and into the light of day to be washed clean of any guilt around them your creations will come bubbling up to the surface like the fountain of youth herself, you see? To release that which has bound you up comes first, then the spring waters of creative ideas flow like Niagara falls. Your light connected to the God Source completes your journey here. As you connect to the Divine Wisdom flow from within you are tapping the inspired flow so that it goes from a trickle to continuous loving flow of creative impulses. To be one with Divinity's Magical Love flow daily is the very reason why you arrived here upon beautiful Mother Earth. We give you big celebratory creations and days filled with the pure wonder of the vastness of love born unto you."

Bonus Day 46
Archangel Metatron

"The cycles of rest and play are at the essence of your creative work. As you rest deeply when no inspired action is coming leads you to the deep reservoir of love that resides from within. To not feel inspired to take on more is significant for you, yes? What may be occurring here is a need to reduce your workload in some capacity in order to focus upon that which ultimately feeds your own spirit, body, mind and heart, you see? When we listen to "only" what our audience wants we short circuit our soul's evolutionary process of ultimately becoming more free on all levels of our consciousness. You have done a most excellent job so far with all of your well-spring of ideas you have implemented. We'd like you to look at your "task list" and all the things on your list you think you "should be doing" in order to achieve your dreams. Which of these items feels like a refreshing waterfall that fills your soul up as you perform them? List these items with an "R" next to them for Replenishing. Now ask yourself, which of these items on my agenda makes me feel more depleted afterwards. List these items with a "D" next to them. Allow your items listed with an "R" next to them to float to the top of the to do items. Place your "D" items to the side on a separate list and ask yourself if the "D" – Draining items can be transformed into "R" – Replenishing action steps in anyway shape or form? If they can, ask them how so? If they can, keep them on the to do list and implement them in this invigorating soul replenishing way. For the items that still feel like drains, ask yourself who could help you with them who would feel Replenished by doing them? If no one comes to mind, ask yourself if you absolutely want to complete this item or can you let it go for now to make room for more

Replenishing items that want to help you ascend into higher states of being with your life's work? We want you to know not to be hard on yourself with this process. Let this process free your sense of duty in the world. You are so very loved by us. What remains on your item list will be energized by us so you may effortlessly receive nourishing energy as you have fun with each one."

Bonus Day 47 Archangel Michael

"When you speak to yourself with your inner dialogue be easy on yourself, for there is no higher gift to yourself than what you say to yourself in those moments when you feel no one else is listening. What you think, feel and know matters. We never second guess you, we only offer you golden streams of inspired visions. When you are worried about what you'll get out of your art or creative expression, this may stifle them before they even have a chance of blossoming flowers for you to enjoy. Pretend you have an audience of millions about to view your creative work and this was your last year on earth. What would you say to your audience of millions before you leave the planet? If this was your last work of writing you leave as your gift to mankind, what would you want them to hear and feel deep within them? Go there, be with that golden light wave of all that is good. Ride that golden light beam all the way through till your writing feels like a well spring of golden treasures. As you create from this space, all that is supposed to be said will. There is no need to predetermine your creations end... allow it to take you on a magical journey of wonder each and every day. Looking forward to the journey in this way brings infinite divinely inspired written word journeys ahead."

Go to ArchangelsBless.com to receive FREE Archangel Messages anytime day or night. Ask a question, receive an answer.

About the Author

Kimberly Dawn currently resides in Silver City, New Mexico. She has been called an Angelic Ambassador and is an Energy Medicine Conduit for the Archangels. She helps empathic clients with anxiety, life disappointments, and digestion problems, who are *tired all the time* or have weight gain heal through Archangel Crystal

Light Energy Healing sessions. During the Archangel Crystal Light Energy Healing sessions the Archangels are able to connect her clients back up to their Divine Soul's Calling and Life Purpose Blueprint so they feel more peaceful, connected and clear again.

You may enjoy learning more about the "Stay Motivated Archangel Crystal Light Energy Healings" on Monday nights. To find out more go to ArchangelsBless.com and click on "Stay Motivated" on the home page.

Bringing You Peace, Healing, Joy & Profound Blessings

Message from the healing team that work with the Archangels during the Archangel Crystal Light Energy Healings

The healing team that work through the Archangels wanted me to channel something tonight and here it is... Woah, I have simplified what I do, but obviously they wanted me to type about the intricacies of what THEY do!

"We are bringing this transmission through Kimberly this evening as an unexpected gift. We asked her to type it because we wanted to bring in a more accurate description of the detail and intricacy in which we work on every single one of her clients as she turns on the crystal lights and places their name or photo under the lights with them receiving the healing from their location while meditating.

What is difficult to understand because it cannot be seen with the physical eye, only the 3rd eye from the spiritual mind is that a healing platform or bridge, if you will, has been created so that "light body specialists" from the other side, who are reaching you through an inter dimensional doorway via a protected space are helping to repair and restore the body's natural restorative wisdom with advanced light techniques. It is no small task to come through and assist in the healing process of the human body like this, yet because of the light grid work that has been done in another time and place and with permission of a person's soul, God and the Angelic Counsels of light the healing can be done with precision.

The energetic pain grids in the body that contribute to pain create a build-up or a layer on the outside of the auric field like scar tissue. Often when we work on the energy bodies we remove this scar tissue energetically in order for more healing frequencies of light and geometric codes of light that repair actual tissue to reach the actual injury inside the body.

When these layers build up because they have never been energetically removed, such as around the heart area, then heart pain occurs. The heart cannot draw in enough prana or life force energy into the system to essentially heal itself through revitalizing its own molecules.

The heart is an especially sensitive area. When one's heart has too much hardening of the arteries and then surgery is performed on the physical heart, this helps tremendously, yet often times the hardened arteries return causing the heart to work harder than normal to do its job. The energetic scar tissue also needs to be removed in layers.

We cannot remove too many layers at once due to needing to shield the auric field from tearing and allowing time to heal in between treatments.

Depending on how severe someone's health

issues are and the layers of scar tissue build up grids that are in the auric field the issue may need a 2, 3 or 4-fold application of healing. The first being energetic healing such as the kind we perform (focused precision light body surgery from the other side), the second being any herbal medicinal needs addressed buy a qualified herbalist, third the dietary changes that can be made to assist the body with helping itself heal and fourth being any western medical care needed to treat any acute or chronic conditions in the body.

To address healing from a 4-fold initiative or a multiplatform approach helps the body's natural rejuvenation system and often times reverse the aging process all together.

What helps the body begin the process of healing itself is by simply reducing the amount of toxic overload the body already has. Eating more organic foods, super foods, herbal formulas that are right for you and doing light cleanses helps the body to release all the toxic overload it is carrying.

What we see all too often is a sort of dumping of

waste products inside the tissues and the cells of the body. It is likened to if you thought you were dumping your kitchen trash waste into the local landfill but turning to look outside your kitchen window and realizing all the waste has never left, it is still inside your backyard overflowing onto the sides of the house and back in through the doors.

The body wants to purify itself. The body wants to heal the toxic overload that happens. Once you assist the body in the ways for mentioned the body's toxic stress levels begin reducing. What has life in it brings your body to life more. What has very little life force energy in it such as boxed or canned goods ends up deadening and polluting the body systems, organs, heart and lymph nodes. The world has solved some of its hunger and famine problems with packaged and processed foods, but not without a very high price.

There is also electrical circuitry or channels of energy that run all throughout your light body. There are millions and millions of them. If we gave you a glow light that allowed you to see them, you would see that some of your circuitry areas are not firing correctly. There are circuitry issues happening in many people's electrical currents that run through their bodies. This is why sometimes there are areas of the body that become numb or where numbing sensations happen.

In these areas the electric circuitry needs to be repaired.

This also cannot happen on one go around with only one Archangel Crystal Light Session as it may take quite a few. Kimberly's right calf and S-1 nerve running through her right leg had light circuitry issues after having her L-5 disk removed during back surgery. This has been repaired by us. Sometimes it takes several sessions in a row to fire up again the electrical circuits in any given area to keep them going. Like retraining a muscle, it takes working out the muscle to build it up again. Muscle training is likened to the electrical circuitry work that we do.

We have very specific electrical circuit repair specialists who come in during an Archangel

Crystal Light Energy Healing Session that repair and revitalize the electrical circuitry in the body. What causes the electrical circuits to weaken can be any number of things such as the quality of food one eats, traumas that have happened in that person's life, x-rays and cat scans can also effect the electrical current pathways inside the body, thus causing them to misfire or deaden. How many shocks or life scares that person has had and also not being grounded and connecting one's feet to Mother Earth's natural grounding loving healing energy. By discharging one's positive (or static charge or build up) inside the body and refilling with Mother Earth's fuel, negative ions and a negative healing charge enter the feet and go all the way up to the brain, which enhances brain functions with improved memory and better focus.

We'd like to conclude this transmission through Kimberly by saying sleep disturbances and sleep patterns can also be improved from receiving the Archangel Crystal Light Healing Sessions. We could go on for hours and months even with dissertations of the precision of light body, spiritual, mental, emotional and physical body repairs that our team of specialists do for Kimberly's clients.

This work is protected and sanctioned through Kimberly because she has agreed on a soul level to be a bridge for us and our team of specialists. We thank you for taking the time to read or listen to this transmission. To bring more fortification of healing to you is our honor and a great privilege. Forever at your service. Namaste'."

Sign up for FREE Archangel Messages... Ask a question, get an answer by going to: http://archangelsbless.com/

27794217R00074

Printed in Great Britain
by Amazon